RAILWAY MOODS

THE SEVERN VALLEY RAILWAY

MIKE HEATH

HALSGROVE

First published in Great Britain in 2005

British Library Cataloguing-in-Publication Data
A CIP record for this title is available from the British Library

ISBN 1 84114 444 4

HALSGROVE
Halsgrove House
Lower Moor Way
Tiverton, Devon EX16 6SS
Tel: 01884 243242
Fax: 01884 243325
email: sales@halsgrove.com
website: www.halsgrove.com

Printed and bound by D'Auria Industrie Grafiche Spa, Italy

The railway operates all year round and further information can be obtained by calling 01299 401001
or writing to The Severn Valley Railway, The Railway Station, Bewdley, Worcestershire, DY12 1BG.
Alternatively you can visit the website at www.svr.co.uk

INTRODUCTION

The 'original' Severn Valley Line, constructed between 1858 and 1862, was part of Britain's rail network as a through route, linking Hartlebury, near Droitwich in Worcestershire with Shropshire's county town Shrewsbury. A link to Kidderminster was constructed by the Great Western Railway in 1878 giving a direct route up the valley for trains from the West Midlands industrial area. The line provided an essential service for the local population until the 1930s when major improvement in roads and the competition from motor lorries hit rail freight traffic hard. During the 1950s a rapid increase in family car ownership and the resultant decline in passenger traffic meant that the line's fate was sealed. In 1963 it fell victim to the national closure plan, although the coal mines at Alveley used rail transport until 1969 and a passenger service between Kidderminster and Bewdley struggled on until 1970.

There the story would have ended, but for a group of local railway enthusiasts who, in 1965, had formed the Severn Valley Railway Society and set about raising money to purchase the section of line from Bridgnorth to Alveley. They then tackled the restoration of the track and succeeded in reopening the line from Bridgnorth to Hampton Loade in May 1970. The cessation of coal traffic from Alveley Colliery and passenger traffic to Bewdley paved the way for the Society to extend its own services. Highley was reached in April 1974, Bewdley the following month. At this time part of the line between Bewdley and Kidderminster was still in British Rail ownership and not available for purchase until 1982. Over £370,000 was raised to buy this remaining section and develop a new SVR passenger station at Kidderminster which was opened to passenger traffic on 30 July 1984, completing a 16 mile long preserved railway.

The Severn Valley Railway of today follows the meandering course of the River Severn from the Shropshire town of Bridgnorth in the north, through the villages of Hampton Loade, Highley, and Arley to the Worcestershire town of Bewdley where it leaves the river and heads east to terminate in Kidderminster.

What follows is a personal photographic journey capturing this fascinating line by day and by night, as it passes through a varied and mostly unspoilt landscape, calling off at the beautifully restored country stations each of which retains its own unique timeless charm and from which one can gain access to local villages and riverside walks. The scenery on offer is only really available to rail passengers and walkers as there is limited road access to the area.

I was first attracted to this railway in the early 1980s by an advertisement for their autumn gala at which 13 locomotives would be working. The combination of so many different locomotives hauling trains through such a beautiful landscape was perfect for my developing photography hobby. It was also a wonderful day out for my then young family. Needless to say many return visits have been made, more recently accompanied by my younger son, Karl, who has allowed me to use some of his own excellent photographs in this album. Thank you Karl.

The current SVR timetable pamphlet declares the railway as 'a line for all seasons'. I could not agree more!

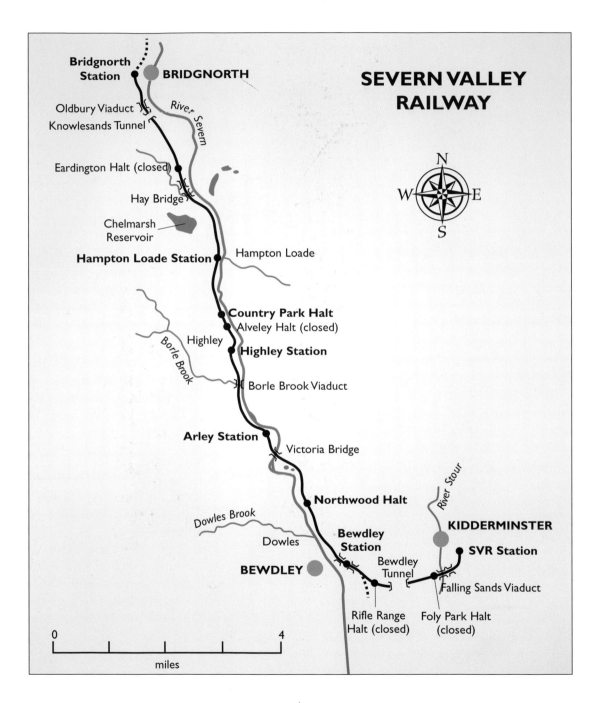

SEVERN VALLEY RAILWAY

Bridgnorth Station

BRIDGNORTH

River Severn

Oldbury Viaduct
Knowlesands Tunnel

Eardington Halt (closed)

Hay Bridge

Chelmarsh Reservoir

Hampton Loade Station

Hampton Loade

Country Park Halt
Alveley Halt (closed)

Borle Brook

Highley

Highley Station

Borle Brook Viaduct

Arley Station

Victoria Bridge

River Stour

Northwood Halt

Dowles Brook

Dowles

KIDDERMINSTER

Bewdley Station

SVR Station

BEWDLEY

Bewdley Tunnel

Falling Sands Viaduct

Rifle Range Halt (closed)

Foly Park Halt (closed)

N
W   E
S

0   4
miles

No need for a television screen or digital monitor as passengers at Bridgnorth are clearly directed to the next 'all stations' departure for Kidderminster.

The town of Bridgnorth grew up around its castle and later became a river port on the Severn, giving rise to its split level development, with Low Town on the river bank, and High Town on the sandstone cliff above. Meandering paths, steps and a cliff railway link the two.

Bridgnorth Station is connected to High Town by the new footbridge, seen here in the background, which was opened in 1994, a replacement for the original that had stood from 1895 until 1976. On the cliff top stands the remains of Bridgnorth Castle and the tower of St Mary's church.

This is usually my first port of call when visiting the railway and where the Severn Valley line's preservation activities started back in 1965.

Beyond the platforms is the railway's locomotive works and shed. On gala weekends the yard comes alive with large numbers of locomotives being prepared for their day's work.

At the start of the day locomotive cleaning is carried out by enthusiasts of all ages under appropriate supervision. This photograph was taken in 1984 since when Health and Safety regulations have restricted access to the yard and works for the general public, making it difficult to capture such scenes today. However the SVR provide access for public viewing during most special event weekends.

The water tanks are then replenished.

With the boiler at working pressure, and steam forcing its way out of the cylinder drain cocks, the locomotive eases out of the yard.

The taking of the previous photograph was followed by a mad dash along the platform in order to take this shot at the signal gantry. My hopes were that the gentleman walking the track would pass by quickly and therefore not appear in the photograph. My initial disappointment was later overcome when this photograph won the Transport Category in a photography magazine's Photographer of The Year competition. The judges citing the careful placing of the railwayman in the foreground being a significant feature!

On leaving the yard the locomotive has to run beyond the points and signals that control all movements into the station. This procedure is captured here against an autumn-tinted background.

Departure time draws near and the footplate crew await the 'right-away' from the guard.

The journey commences on a beautiful summer's day.

Opposite: The Autumn Gala usually features all night running giving the opportunity to capture steam after dark. The glow from the firebox illuminates the footplate and the light from the platform lamps reflects along the side of this night train's carriages.

A departing train heads south away from this panoramic scene, taken from the Bridgnorth by-pass.

A demonstration freight train is on its way, on an overcast summer's day, and will run alongside the meandering course of the River Severn, seen in the background, for most of its route.

The first 1½ miles of the journey is at a gradient of 1 in 100 up to the line's summit at Eardington. Once passed, the train coasts downhill towards Eardington Halt, as here where a Lancastrian visitor, locomotive 42765 from the East Lancashire Railway at Bury, cruises past.

Located some distance from the village of the same name, Eardington Halt seems quite remote. Initially built to serve two ironworks, the latter years of British Rail ownership saw fishermen providing most of the custom. In the early years of preservation when the SVR commenced services between Bridgnorth and Hampton Loade the halt was used as an intermediate stopping place with watering facilities. Nowadays a small group of volunteers maintain the halt, and on some gala weekends provide watering facilities for photographers!

In 1970 the SVR restarted services from Bridgnorth and for the first four years Hampton Loade was the southern terminus for passenger operations. The station itself is located in the hamlet of Hampton, Hampton Loade being situated on the opposite side of the river. An historic ferry maintains a link, operating from a landing stage just down the lane from the station.

Opposite: The tranquillity of a country station is about to be disturbed by the arrival of the next train to Kidderminster.

Again a keen group of volunteer staff have repaired, restored and maintained the station in superb condition. The many pieces of platform furniture and relics that have been collected complete the scene in this photograph taken at dusk

A step into the booking office is a step back in time.

Just behind platform two is the Paddock Railway where steam locomotives of a much smaller scale can be viewed alongside their full-sized counterparts.

Whilst trains pass at this point during the summer, narrow road access restricts the number of visitors arriving by car. The tranquil country-station atmosphere is therefore maintained. This is the view south – note the closeness of the river which can be seen through the trees beyond the partially-restored vintage coach.

A short demonstration freight clatters along heading for the next station, Highley.

Opposite: At the 1997 Spring Gala a walk along the riverbank south of Hampton Loade revealed this location where low-angled photographs of locomotives pulling away from the station could be taken.

For much of the journey the river is never far away affording passengers great views whatever the season.

A colourful springtime welcome awaits the train, once the signal permits it to enter the station.

(Photo: Karl Heath)

31

The railway has recently introduced a 'Severn Valley in Bloom' weekend at the end of July, to highlight the beautiful station gardens and floral displays.

Many are the times that I have sat on a platform bench, surrounded by the fragrant tubs and hanging baskets, consuming purchases from the station's excellent refreshment kiosk.

It is difficult to believe, but in its former life Highley Station was the focal point for up to four local collieries with which it was linked by rail, cable inclines and aerial runways. Unfortunately, like many country stations it is located a mile away from the village it was meant to serve and therefore, from the 1930s, when competition from buses, which started their journeys from the village centre, commenced, passenger numbers began to decline.

With his arm aloft the Highley signalman prepares to exchange tokens with the footplate crew. They will receive that allowing them to continue to Arley whilst at the same time releasing the token for the section from Hampton Loade.

The station area has been beautifully restored by another band of dedicated volunteers with many railway period facilities provided. Alongside the signal box is a loading gauge. These were installed so that railway staff could ensure that loaded wagons leaving the goods yard would pass safely under bridges.

Opposite: Shunting demonstrations are a feature of special event weekends.

Once a year the role played by working horses in the early days of the railways is celebrated at numerous locations along the line. At Highley shunting using literal horse power is recreated.

Period vehicles can often be seen at, or between, stations providing different photographic opportunities. This vintage coach, which I believe is a Midland Red C1 built in 1948 by Duple, makes a splendid sight heading away from Highley.

(Photo: Karl Heath)

Back at the station the train is also heading south on a spring afternoon.

The next stage of the journey, towards Arley, continues alongside the river through an alternating landscape of shallow cuttings and low embankments. Like most other preserved railways the SVR brings in visiting locomotives to supplement its own fleet from time to time. In 1992 Bulleid-built 'Battle of Britain' class locomotive no. 34072 named *257 Squadron* was hired in from the Swanage Railway in Dorset.

By way of contrast the locomotive seen here, scurrying towards Arley, has been part of the home fleet since 1972, and is no stranger to travelling through beautiful scenery. No. 3442 named *The Great Marquess* was one of a number of locomotives built by the London and North Eastern Railway, for use on one of the most scenic railway routes in Britain – the West Highland line from Glasgow to Fort William and Mallaig in Scotland, where it worked from 1938 until the end of 1959.

The riverside footpath from Highley to Arley is joined at right angles by a number of secondary paths that cross the railway. This photograph was taken at one of these crossing points. The driver can be seen looking to ensure the road ahead is clear and I will have raised my arm to confirm my awareness of the approaching train.

The countryside along this section is particularly unspoilt as the line passes through an area of mixed farming with riverside meadows. The footplate crew need to be aware of a number of farm track crossings along this stretch. The river can be seen just behind the locomotive.

Opposite: A streamlined locomotive, built for high speeds on the East Coast main line looks somewhat out of place trundling into a country station. But there is no doubting the elegance of Sir Nigel Gresley's design of the A4 class locomotives represented here by No. 60009 *Union of South Africa.*

Arley village is located on the opposite riverbank to its station, and accessed via the footbridge, seen in the background, which was erected in 1973 as a replacement for an ageing cable ferry. The locomotive is on the final approach to the station.

Arley Station is another picturesque location, and the busiest country station on the line, due in part to the existence of large car parks located on either bank of the river. It achieved fame in 1997 when the BBC chose it as the base for the situation comedy 'Oh Doctor Beeching' when it took on the guise of the fictitious village of Hatley.

Visitors calling in the waiting room can look at an old photograph depicting an abandoned and near derelict station in 1971. The magnificent condition of the station, as seen in this photograph, results from the hard work of yet another small group of dedicated volunteers. This was taken in 1999 when work to replace the platform awning was underway.

Whilst the main station building at Arley is original, the signal box was imported from Yorton, near Whitchurch in Shropshire and erected on the same site as the original, which had been demolished when the original line closed.

A general view taken looking north from the road bridge, which is also used by passengers to change platforms. The passing loop here is one of the main crossing points for trains travelling up and down the valley.

Alternate examples of steam traction often recreate cameo scenes of the past in the station yard during special event weekends

A railwayman's view of a typical 'mixed' train about to depart on a very damp day. Locomotive No. 813 is worthy of mention as it is over 100 years old, having been built by Hudswell Clarke in Leeds in 1900.

Opposite: A passenger's view of a typical 'local' train, about to depart.

If you descend the hill from the station to the riverside, a short walk south takes you to the Victoria Bridge. The railway itself approaches the bridge on a small embankment. This photograph taken from the riverside path.

(Photo: Karl Heath)

The same location captured from higher up the valley.

Victoria Bridge was built in 1861 and at that time its single span of 200 feet was the longest in the world. Needless to say it is the largest engineering structure on the SVR. The locomotive pictured also has an interesting history. LMR No. 600 *Gordon* was built in 1943 for overseas service, but never actually served overseas. It was sent to the Longmoor Military Railway in Hampshire and spent most of its working life there. When the base closed in the late 1960s the SVR provided the location to preserve it. You may also note the resemblance to the locomotive of the same name in the Reverend Awdry's Thomas the Tank Engine books.

In 1994 the bridge received extensive repairs following which nearly 700 gallons of paint were used to restore it to the original colour seen here.

Once across the bridge the line passes through Eymore Wood cutting emerging alongside Trimpley Reservoir.

Opposite: From Victorian times Birmingham's water requirements have been served via an 80-mile long pipeline from the Elan Reservoir in Wales. Trimpley Reservoirs were constructed to hold water, extracted from the River Severn, for use at times of peak demand when water is pumped into the Elan Aqueduct to supplement the supply.

Passing the same location on a wet autumn morning is the 'mixed' train last seen about to leave Arley.

Opposite: On a lovely summer's day the train is about a mile from Bewdley and passing the point where the former line from Tenbury Wells and Woofferton joined from the left of the picture, and ran parallel all the way to Bewdley Station.

(Photo: Karl Heath)

This section of track is clearly visible from the other side of the river, particularly in winter when the trees are bare.

And in spring, as here, where the passing of a Great Western Railway vintage train, during the Spring Gala of 2003, is photographed.

A signalman's view of the northern approach to Bewdley Station which is across the seven-arched Wribbenhall Viaduct.

Opposite: The B4194 running north out of Bewdley also provides a good vantage point.

The approach as seen from the platforms. The locomotive is about to pass the hook and netting that would once have sent and received post bags via a travelling post office train.

Bewdley Station, with its three platforms, is the largest on the line, maintaining an atmosphere of a small town junction station. British Rail passenger services finished in 1970 when an infrequent diesel service to Kidderminster was withdrawn. Four years later the new SVR Company purchased the buildings, land and track enabling its own services, which up to then had terminated at Hampton Loade, to be extended to Bewdley.

The main entrance to the station, and a reminder of a time when the station porter could leave his bike leaning on the wall outside, in full expectation that it would still be there when his shift had finished!

Passengers standing on platform one have a panoramic view over the predominantly Georgian rooftops of historic Bewdley.

The train for Kidderminster arrives in platform two; crossing with the Bridgnorth-bound train standing in platform one.

Opposite: A gala night time scene as a trio of locomotives stand alongside a very wet platform.

In 2002 the railway organised a night time photographic session with locomotives being positioned at various locations within the station limits.

Photographing steam at night is a favourite pastime of mine, and my younger son Karl, as this selection of shots taken at this event no doubt show!

At night, scenes from days gone by can be recreated, as twenty-first-century backgrounds are hidden under a cloak of darkness.

There's always time for a brew before the next freight train pulls in for unloading! A 'Heavy Horse Weekend' scene, in the goods yard.

The final section of the SVR seen today was opened to passenger services on 30 July 1984, since when south-bound departures such as this one, from platform three, could be recorded.

(Photo: Karl Heath)

A Kidderminster-bound train eases past the water tower as it hauls its train away from platform two.

The safe operation of the railway relies on the work carried out by the Signal and Telecommunications Department. Evidence of their work can be seen in the background with the array of signals around Bewdley South signal box.

The West Midlands Safari Park is located alongside the line just south of Bewdley and passengers can catch a glimpse of several forms of wildlife running free within the security fencing and hoardings.

Other forms of wildlife, such as railway photographers, thought by some to be equally unusual, can also be seen trackside.

Opposite: Those shadowy figures were actually participants in a photographer's charter organised by the 'Friends of the locomotive *Hagley Hall*', to raise funds for the restoration of that particular locomotive. This is the photograph that they were waiting to take.

Pictured here is one of a number of 'regal' visitors to the SVR. Former London, Midland and Scottish Railways locomotive 6233 *Duchess of Sutherland* passes the safari park during the Autumn Gala of 2002.

Opposite: This next section of track that runs from the southern boundary of the safari park to the entrance of Bewdley tunnel runs along an embankment and the lie of the adjacent land affords panoramic views with many photographic opportunities.

Overhanging tree branches combine with the grass verge and fencing to form a natural frame for this passing vintage train.

On a hot summer's day the streamlined locomotive *Union of South Africa* races towards Bewdley tunnel.

(Photo: Karl Heath)

The final approach into Kidderminster runs alongside the main line, seen here to the left. In the middle distance on the right, identified by the curved roof, is the railway's new carriages shed, constructed during 1999/2000 with the aid of Heritage Lottery Funding.

Opposite: By way of contrast, on a gorgeous autumn morning, a typical Great Western Railway branch line train trundles past the point where Rifle Range Halt once stood. Between 1905 and 1920 this was used by Yeomanry volunteers training on the heathland alongside the railway. Evidence of the range still exists today, but no trace of the halt remains

The SVR station at Kidderminster, designated 'Kidderminster Town' gives the appearance of a period building but was actually built from new on the site of the former British Rail goods yard alongside the main rail network's own station. Opened in 1986 the buildings are based on original Great Western Railway designs and incorporate all the usual facilities including a traditional W.H.Smith sales kiosk.

The cobbled forecourt is supplemented with equally dated roadside signage and structures and, on 'Heavy Horse Weekend', horses of the mechanical kind. Of note is the Bundy clock which was an instrument used by tram drivers who would enter their times at various locations, thus ensuring good timekeeping.

Ready for departure as shadows lengthen on a clear crisp January afternoon.

Opposite: It's dusk on a 'Santa Special' day, and all eyes are on locomotive movements at the north end of the platforms.

In keeping with the station buildings, the signal box, which controls all locomotive movements in and out of Kidderminster, was also built to a Great Western Railway design and opened in 1988. A fully laden 'Santa Special' departs for Santa's Grotto at Arley.

Opposite: The previous photograph was taken from the footbridge seen here in the background. Beyond is the signal box with a clear view of the signal gantry, with which it controls access to Kidderminster Town Station.

Shortly after leaving Kidderminster the railway crosses Falling Sands Viaduct, which spans both the River Stour and the Stafford and Worcestershire Canal.

A train emerges from the 480-feet long Bewdley tunnel and into the spring sunshine on the return journey to Bridgnorth.

Recreating a typical branch line scene, a 'local' train passes the site of the former Rifle Range Halt.

Opposite: The railway carries in excess of 240,000 passengers a year and therefore needs to maintain a substantial fleet of coaches to provide adequate accommodation. Their fleet, where possible, is arranged in matching rakes, such as here where a train of 'blood and custard' coaches typical of British Railways in the 1950s, is drifting downhill towards Bewdley.

This demonstration freight train is passing the West Midlands Safari Park on the outskirts of Bewdley.

Opposite: Another royal visitor, in the shape of former London Midland and Scottish Railway's locomotive no. 6201 *Princess Elizabeth*.

In high season Bewdley Station sees regular arrivals and departures. This view of a busy platform one is taken from the footbridge.

Waiting for the milk train, a timeless scene.

The siding at Bewdley is used for the stabling of the operational locomotives rostered to haul the first departures from Kidderminster. Here a collection of tank engines simmer under a threatening sky.

Opposite: *Gordon*, the big blue engine, on an overnight stop.

'This is the Night Mail'. Memories of W.H. Auden's poem were rekindled on a damp October night in 2001 when, courtesy of a 'Friends of the locomotive *Hagley Hall*' arranged a night photography event. A train comprising a number of former Royal Mail coaches was posed at locations around the station.

Another feature of the evening was the period uniforms worn by members of the organising group of volunteers.

Working steam locomotives, beautifully restored stations with their signboards, evocative artefacts such as hanging baskets, poster boards, milk churns and luggage trolleys, with uniformed staff in attendance, all combine to create the complete Severn Valley experience.

Opposite: Floodlighting emphasises the locomotive wheels and motion in this rear three-quarter portrait.

With trains crossing at Bewdley, Autumn Gala night time passengers have a choice of destinations.

Opposite: Nightime passengers make themselves comfortable as the footplate crew check the gauges by the light of the fire.

Progress north can only continue when the south-bound train has arrived alongside the platform, surrendering its single line token to the signalman as it passes the signal box.

Trains leaving Bewdley immediately cross Bewdley North (or Wribbenhall) Viaduct allowing passengers to enjoy the commanding view over the streets of Bewdley, referred to earlier on our journey south.

Branch line weekend and the SVR has hired in an autocoach and suitably fitted small tank engine to recreate a single coach push-pull train, commonplace on many local branches in the days of steam. Autocoaches were fitted, at one end, with controls linked to the locomotive regulator, brakes and whistle allowing them to be driven from within the coach while the fireman remained on the footplate to maintain the fire. This allowed the train to trundle up and down a branch line without the locomotive having to run round at each end of the line.

A fisherman's view of a double headed train powering its way north, towards Arley.

For about a mile north of Bewdley the railway formation was double track width to accommodate a second branch line, controlled from Bewdley. The train here is pounding past the point where this other line diverged to follow a course that took it across the river and on to Tenbury Wells and Woofferton. The sloping trackbed of this branch is in the foreground.

(Photo: Karl Heath)

The Tenbury Wells branch crossed the River Severn by means of Dowles Bridge the piers of which remain intact, providing an interesting foreground as trains pass by on the preserved Severn Valley line.

A feature of photographers' charter trains is that, at a range of locations, the train stops allowing the participants to disembark to take up their positions. The locomotive then sets back, as seen here, alongside Trimpley Reservoir, to perform a number of run pasts.

On most operating Sundays a dining service is available on the lunchtime departure from Kidderminster. Diners on this particular 'Severn Valley Limited' train can enjoy a crystal clear view across Trimpley Reservoir as they pass slowly by.

In late summer 1993 a north bound train glides across Victoria Bridge on the approach to Arley.

By the time this next photograph was taken, some seven years later in the first spring of the new millennium, the bridge has received major refurbishment, and a repaint into its original colour. The riverbank has also seen some clearance work.

High summer 1990, and, with Eymore Wood forming a rich green backdrop, a mixed rake train comprising both passenger and freight stock, starts to pull away from the bridge.

Opposite: Winter 2004, and the same location seen in a totally different light.

Both north- and south-bound mid-week summer service trains use the main platform at Arley affording photographers the opportunity to capture the 'full side' of Bridgnorth-bound trains entering the station.

Despite the driver's headgear, this is not Thunderbird 6! It is in fact a demonstration freight train making its way to Bewdley. Of personal interest are the two young lads pressed against the fencing. They are my sons Darren and Karl whose ages, at the time of compiling this book, are twenty-three and nineteen respectively!

Attention to detail is paid to all aspects of railway preservation on the SVR with authentic liveries applied to all rolling stock. For example the van nearest the camera has been painted into the internal user colours of its former owners, Cadbury's.

The first freight train of the day coasts past the restored cattle dock on the approach to Highley Station.

A seemingly deserted station helps to maintain a virtually timeless scene.

Opposite: The single line tokens have been exchanged and the signalman is returning to his box to release the signal that will allow the train to continue its journey north.

Railway preservation is not just about steam locomotives. It includes preserving, as far as possible, the way railway life was in the days of steam. In this picture, with the sidings full of goods wagons, the shunter eavesdrops on the banter between the signalman and footplate crew as the token is handed over. In years gone by this scene would have been repeated many times over, at stations all over the country.

Time for the off, and a final look back along the platform as the locomotive takes the strain.

A few moments later, and with steam to spare, the train forges away from the station.

A fine sight as an impression of a main line express is recreated between Highley and Hampton Loade.

Station staff police the foot crossing as a crowded platform at Hampton Loade watches the next departure to Bridgnorth.

(Photo: Karl Heath)

It may not suit everybody, but to an enthusiast there can be no finer view from a bedroom window!

Vintage Great Western Railway carriages superbly restored are shown off to good effect from this low vantage point. The rear two are handsome 'Toplight' coaches so named after the small oblong windows fitted at high level. Hundreds of these were built between 1908 and 1922.

Opposite: Between Hampton Loade and Eardington is Sterns Cottage, a location infamous for a landslip which has led to a speed restriction on this section, in place from the day the line was built. With a 1 in 100 gradient to climb shortly after, locomotives have to work hard as they accelerate away.

Locations where locomotives have to work hard are always popular with photographers and here at Hay Bridge, on the climb away from Sterns, is no exception. Unfortunately on hot summer days the exhaust can be barely detectable.

But on a cold spring day a totally different effect is created.

(Photo: Karl Heath)

The shade from a setting sun is lapping against the embankment as the train climbs towards the summit of Eardington Bank.

Opposite: In this traditional view of the same location cotton wool clouds litter the sky as the last light of the day catches this train beavering its way up the bank.

As one train arrives back at Bridgnorth, another is ready to depart. These two locomotives are those seen being cleaned before our pictorial journey began, photographed later that same day back in 1984. Since then the histories of the two locomotives have also headed in opposite directions. 'Black Five' locomotive No. 5000, when due for overhaul, was returned to its owners, the National Railway Museum, where it remains on static display. Whereas former London Midland and Scottish Railway's Jubilee class locomotive No. 5690 *Leander* has continued an active life, between overhauls, and is expected to return to main line specials duties during 2005.

The last train of the day pulls in to platform one and the journey is almost complete. There's just time to visit the sheds.

Nearly all repairs to locomotives based on the Severn Valley Railway are carried out at Bridgnorth. The site boasts a thriving engineering workshop with an extensive range of repair equipment gradually amassed from closed railway workshops and engineering factories and housed in the former goods shed seen at the back of this photograph.

(Photo: Karl Heath)

To the front of the engineering workshop is the engine shed, built in 1977 and capable of housing up to eight locomotives in various stages of renovation, or just in storage. Working locomotives can be seen in the shed yard, and make a fine sight as they 'warm down' at dusk.

It's the end of another journey. The locomotive has uncoupled, and returned to the sheds, where the crew have disposed of the fire and cleaned out the fire grate and smoke box. The tender and water tanks have been refuelled and all left ready for the next trip.